Key Words Sentences

Using High Frequency Vocabulary in Context

She went **back** to get the umbrella.

She went **back** to get the key.

She went **back** to get the ball.

She went **back** to get the wallet.

She went **back** to get the scissors.

She went back to get the broom.

Katy Hill and Mark Hill

Prim-Ed Publishing

www.prim-ed.com

Foreword

Key Word Sentences – Year 2 Book is the third in a series of three books designed to develop a child's high frequency keyword knowledge at Key Stage One, as required by the National Literacy Strategy.

The activities follow a familiar repetitive format intended to support the pupils in writing independently with confidence.

Each page focuses on one high frequency word presented in a simple sentence, helping the child to learn to read and spell each word in context. The key words are scaffolded by other familiar vocabulary to provide differentiated sentences within a child-friendly language. The intention of this series is to provide a way for the child to write independently while exploring and extending their language, as an alternative to rote learning the key words.

The sentences are built on and changed using different nouns, verbs, etc. This enables the child to learn how to use these words through exploring syntax and semantics. Picture clues are used where possible to assist the child with word recognition.

Other books in the series are:
Key Word Sentences – Year R Book
Key Word Sentences – Year 1 Book

Contents

Teachers Notes ii	house 18	pull 38
Curriculum Links iii	how 19	push 39
Record Sheet iv	last 20	saw 40
about 1	laugh 21	school 41
after 2	little 22	should 42
again 3	live 23	sister 43
another 4	lived 24	some 44
back 5	many 25	take 45
because 6	may 26	than 46
been 7	more 27	their 47
brother 8	name 28	these 48
can't 9	new 29	three 49
could 10	next 30	time 50
don't 11	night 31	too 51
door 12	old 32	took 52
first 13	once 33	tree 53
good 14	our 34	water 54
half 15	out 35	way 55
help 16	over 36	who 56
home 17	people 37	would 57

Prim-Ed Publishing www.prim-ed.com

Key Word Sentences i

Teachers Notes

Key Word Sentences - Year 2 Book contains activities to supplement and develop childrens' knowledge of the National Literacy Strategy high frequency words. The activities will improve their reading, writing, spelling and usage of these words through a familiar context. This familiar repetitive format is intended to support the pupils in writing independently with confidence. Other skills pupils will further develop include language development, sentence construction, grammar and fine motor control.

Words in the Year 1 and 2 books are generally introduced later than those in the Year R book as specified in the Literacy Strategy. Due to publishing constraints, the key words from the Year 1/2 Literacy Strategy word list have been divided into two books for Year 1 and 2. The words in the Year 2 book are generally more difficult than those in the Year 1 book. Children have less writing space and are expected to write or suggest more alternative sentences. The sentences are generally more complex in structure.

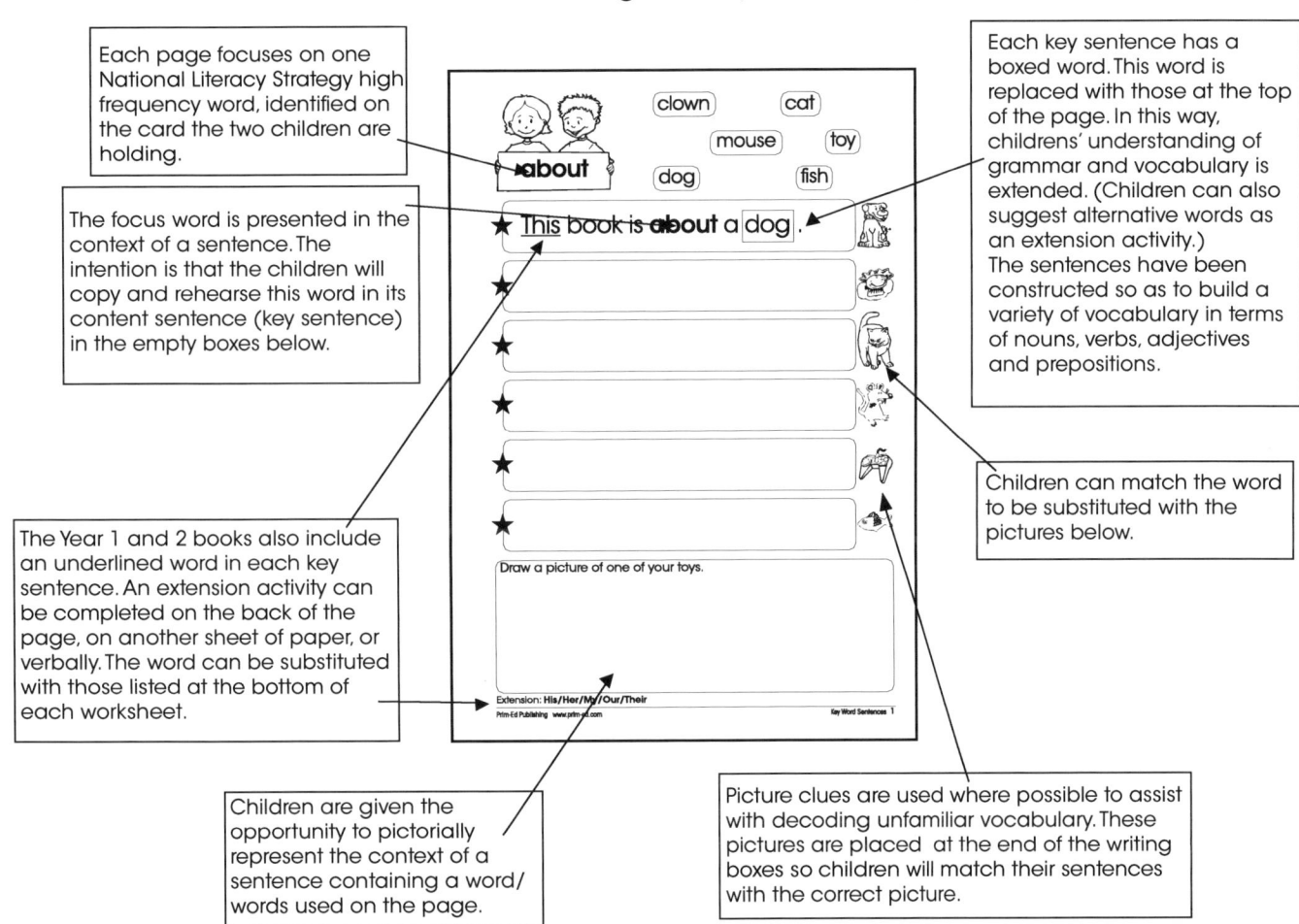

Each page focuses on one National Literacy Strategy high frequency word, identified on the card the two children are holding.

The focus word is presented in the context of a sentence. The intention is that the children will copy and rehearse this word in its content sentence (key sentence) in the empty boxes below.

The Year 1 and 2 books also include an underlined word in each key sentence. An extension activity can be completed on the back of the page, on another sheet of paper, or verbally. The word can be substituted with those listed at the bottom of each worksheet.

Each key sentence has a boxed word. This word is replaced with those at the top of the page. In this way, childrens' understanding of grammar and vocabulary is extended. (Children can also suggest alternative words as an extension activity.) The sentences have been constructed so as to build a variety of vocabulary in terms of nouns, verbs, adjectives and prepositions.

Children can match the word to be substituted with the pictures below.

Children are given the opportunity to pictorially represent the context of a sentence containing a word/words used on the page.

Picture clues are used where possible to assist with decoding unfamiliar vocabulary. These pictures are placed at the end of the writing boxes so children will match their sentences with the correct picture.

The ***Key Word Sentences*** worksheets are intended for use in a variety of settings. They can be used with individual children, small groups or the whole class as part of the Literacy Hour. For the latter, the worksheets can be enlarged to A3 and used as a discussion focus or sentence building task. Individual children can nominate the word to change and the teacher can scribe the sentence.

Individuals will be able to complete the worksheets independently once familiar with the repetitive structure.

Children who have difficulty with fine motor skills can have the worksheets enlarged to A3 to provide more writing space. Teachers/Helpers can also scribe the childrens' sentences with intended meaning (emergent writers).

The ***Key Word Sentences*** series is targeted at early readers in Key Stage One. However, it can also be used for older children with special needs or for ESL/EAL students.

Prim-Ed Publishing www.prim-ed.com **Key Word Sentences ii**

Key Word Sentences
National Literacy Strategy Links

Key Sentences Book	Year	Term	Strand	Content Objectives
Year R Book	R		Word	• read/write letters(s) that represent sound(s): a–z, ch, sh, th • identifying and writing initial and final phonemes in CVC words • read on sight the 45 high frequency words to be taught by the end of YR (NLS, Appendix List 1) • read on sight the words from texts of appropriate difficulty • recognise the critical features of words • extend vocabulary with new words from reading
Year 1 Book	1	1/2/3	Word	• discriminate and segment all three phonemes in CVC words • secure identification, spelling and reading of initial, final and medial letter sounds in simple words • read on sight familiar words • read on sight approximately 90 high frequency words identified for Y1 and Y2 (NLS, Appendix List 1) • recognise the critical features of words • spell common irregular words from NLS, Appendix List 1 • extend vocabulary with new words from reading
Year 2 Book	2	1/2/3	Word	• read on sight and spell all the high frequency words identified for Y1 and Y2 (NLS, Appendix List 1) • spell common irregular words from NLS, Appendix List 1 • extend vocabulary with new words from reading

Literacy Strategy Keyword Record Sheet – Year 2

Name of Child: _____ **Class:** _____

Year 2 NLS Key Word	Child can Read	Child can Spell	Year 2 NLS Key Word	Child can Read	Child can Spell
about			next		
after			night		
again			old		
another			once		
back			our		
because			out		
been			over		
brother			people		
can't			pull		
could			push		
don't			saw		
door			school		
first			should		
good			sister		
half			some		
help			take		
home			than		
house			their		
how			these		
last			three		
laugh			time		
little			too		
live			took		
lived			tree		
many			water		
may			way		
more			who		
name			would		
new					

Prim-Ed Publishing www.prim-ed.com

Key Word Sentences iv

about

clown cat mouse toy dog fish

★ This book is **about** a dog.

★

★

★

★

★

Draw a picture of one of your toys.

Extension: **His / Her / My / Our / Their**

Prim-Ed Publishing www.prim-ed.com

Key Word Sentences 1

after

lunch   school   shopping   tea   playing   swimming

★ I will go after tea.

★

★

★

★

★

Draw a picture of children swimming.

Extension: **run/walk/skip**

Key Word Sentences 2

looking   dancing

playing   shouting

smiling   singing

again

★ Everyone <u>was</u> singing **again**.

★

★

★

★

★

Draw a picture of your friends smiling.

Extension: **sang/looked/danced/played/shouted/smiled**

another

cake   apple   pen   book   biscuit   drink

★ May I <u>have</u> **another** drink ?

★

★

★

★

★

Draw a big birthday cake.

Extension: **take/get/buy/choose**

back

ball scissors wallet broom key umbrella

★ She went **back** to get the umbrella.

★

★

★

★

★

Draw a picture of someone with an umbrella in the rain.

Extension: **find/return/collect**

because

I was wet		I had been swimming.
I was tired	**because**	I had been running.
I was happy		I had been in the bath.
I was hot		I had been playing.

Key Word Sentences 6

been

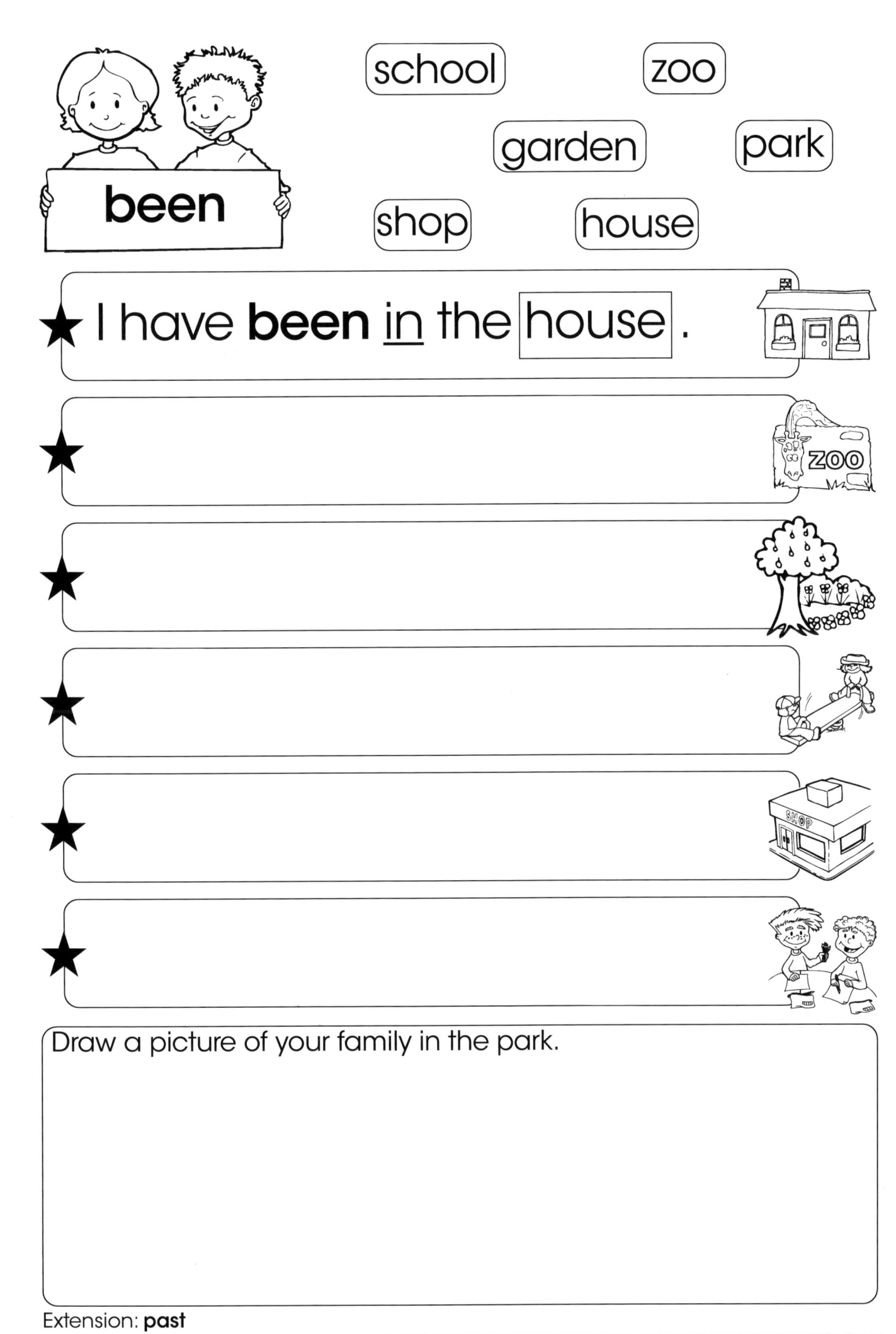

school　　zoo　　garden　　park　　shop　　house

★ I have **been** in the house.

★

★

★

★

★

Draw a picture of your family in the park.

Extension: **past**

Key Word Sentences 7

brother

taller   faster   stronger   older   heavier   smaller

★ My **brother** is smaller than I.

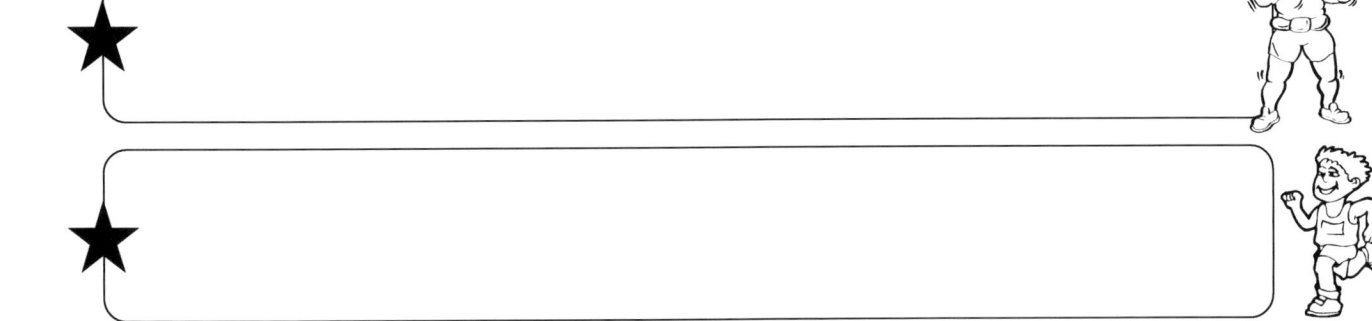

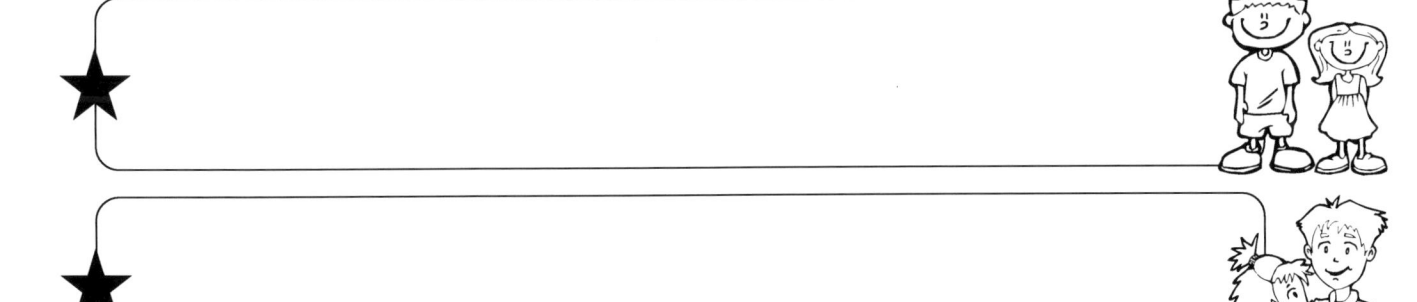

★

★

★

★

★

Draw a picture of someone older than you.

Extension: **friend/dad/sister/mum**

can't

dig, sweep, paint, cook, clean, tidy

★ I **can't** help you to tidy．

★

★

★

★

★

Draw a picture of your tidy bedroom.

Extension: **can/will/won't**

Key Word Sentences 9

could

bag · coat · paintbrush · box · plate · balloon

★ It was the biggest balloon I could find.

★

★

★

★

★

Draw a picture of your coat.

Extension: **smallest/first/last/only/best**

don't

jelly   potato   apples   cabbage   ice-cream   bananas

★ I **don't** like bananas.

★

★

★

★

★

Draw something you like to have for tea.

Extension: **do/would/wouldn't**

Key Word Sentences 11

door

new   glass   broken   big   little   wooden

★ The house has a wooden door.

★

★

★

★

★

Draw a picture of your front door.

Extension: **had**

Key Word Sentences 12

first

plane   cloud
bird   kite
balloon   star

★ I was the **first** person to see a star in the sky.

★

★

★

★

★

Draw a picture of a plane in the sky.

Extension: **last / next / only**

Key Word Sentences 13

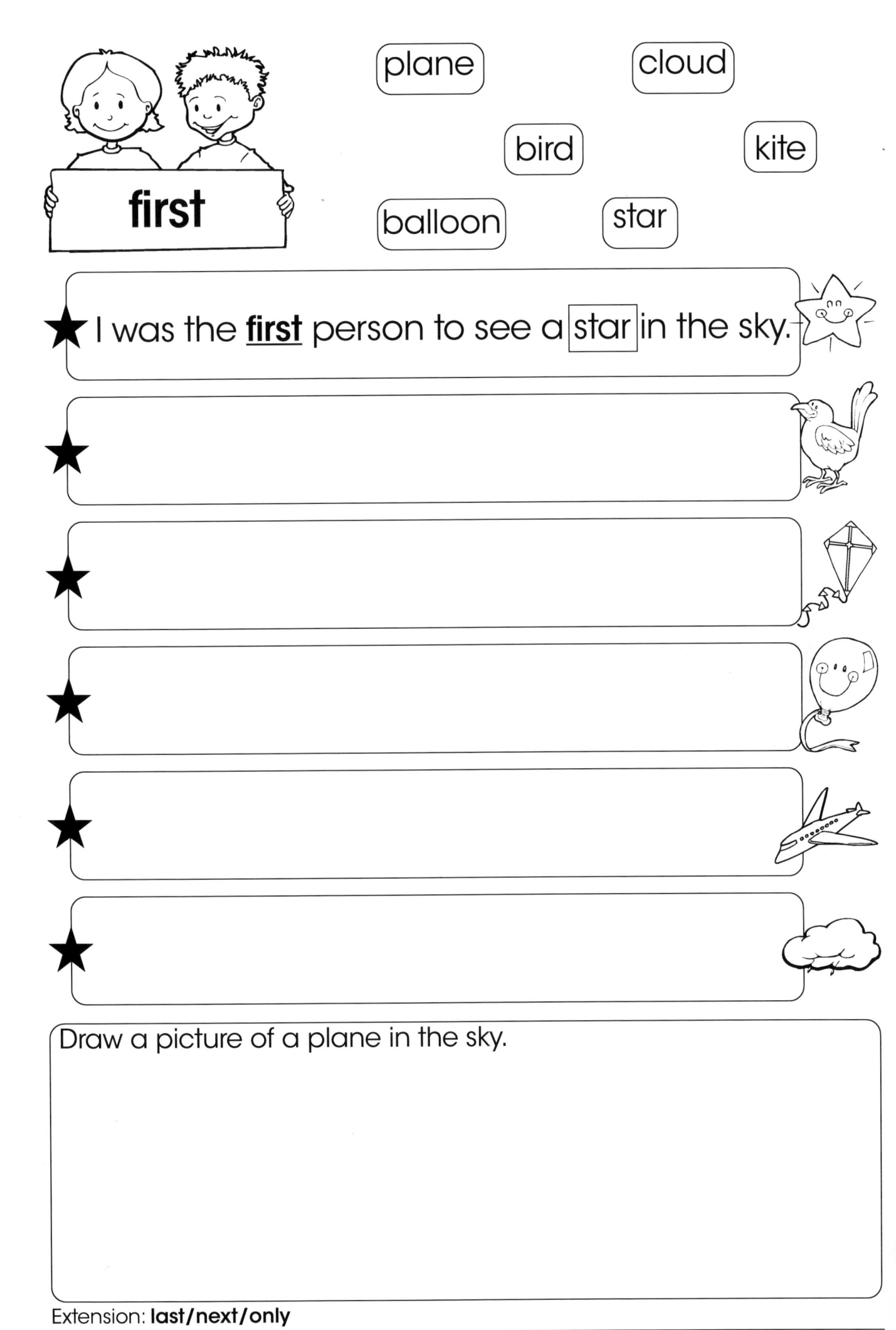

good

dog book computer bike scooter picture

★ My new bike is good.

★

★

★

★

★

Draw a dog playing in the garden.

Extension: **better/best**

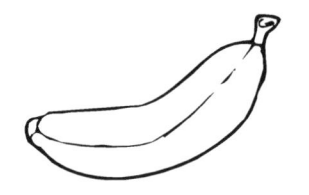

half

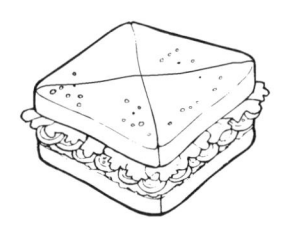

Would you like		of this cake?
Do you want		of my biscuit?
Please may I have	**half**	of that apple?
Can he have		of your banana?
Can you give him		of this sandwich?
Can you give her		of my bun?

★

★

★

★

★

★

Key Word Sentences 15

help

table paint pots cupboard bicycle windows car

★ I <u>want</u> to **help** to clean the windows.

★

★

★

★

★

Draw a picture of you cleaning a car.

Extension: **wanted/would like**

Key Word Sentences 16

home

swing computer bicycle ball slide seesaw

★ At **home**, I have a bicycle.

★

★

★

★

★

Draw a picture of five things you have at home.

Extension: **he has / she has / they have / you have**

Key Word Sentences 17

house

radio   oven   computer   kettle   television   piano

★ In <u>my</u> **house** there is a piano.

★

★

★

★

★

Draw a picture of your house.

Extension: **our/their/this/that/his/her**

how

playground   beach   circus   farm   shop   fire station

★ **How** <u>do</u> you get to the fire station ?

★

★

★

★

★

Draw a picture of a fire engine.

Extension: **would/can/will**

last

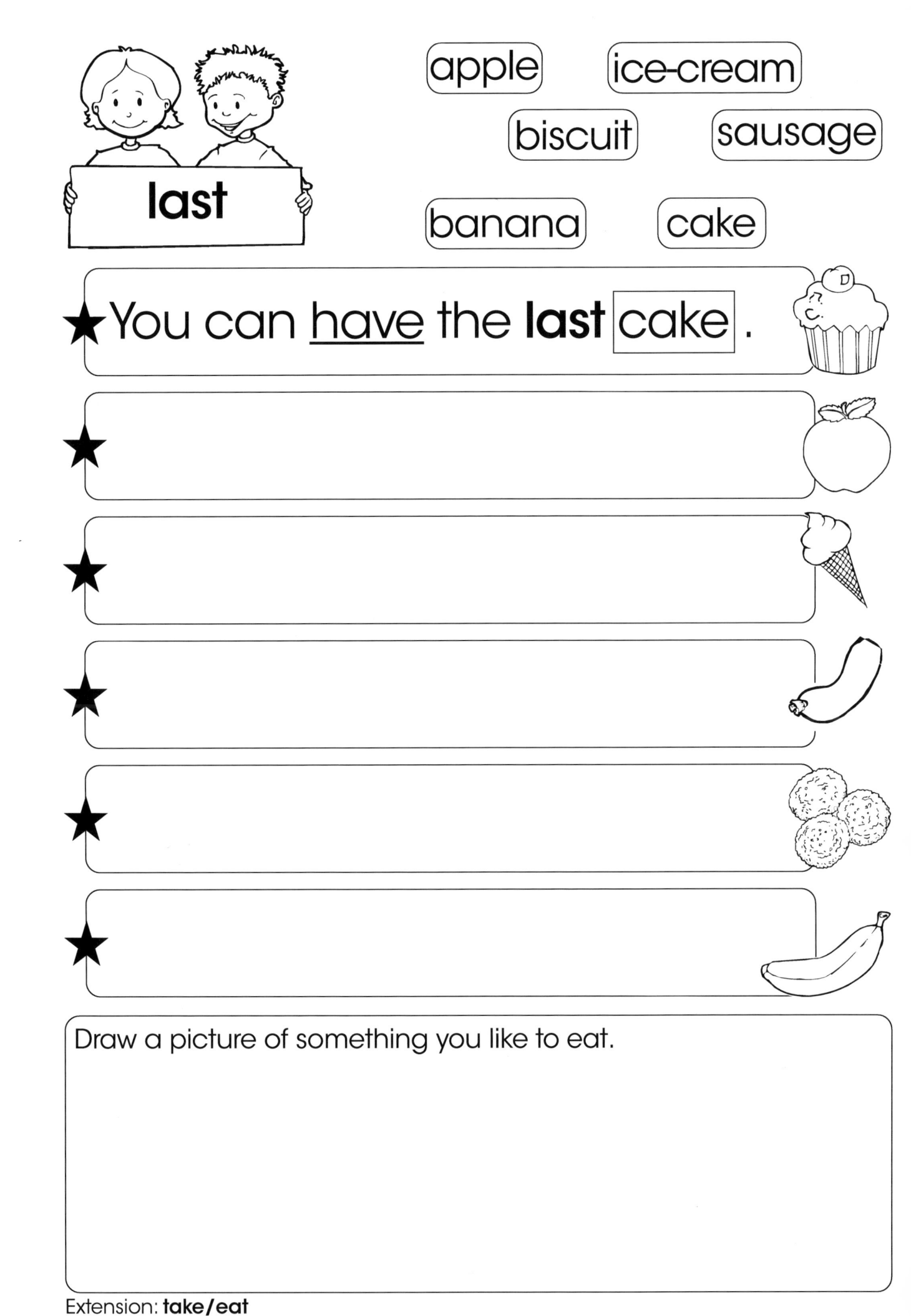

apple   ice-cream   biscuit   sausage   banana   cake

★ You can have the **last** cake.

★

★

★

★

★

Draw a picture of something you like to eat.

Extension: **take/eat**

laugh

balloon   cat   joke   dog   picture   dad

★ My dad makes us **laugh**.

★

★

★

★

★

Draw a funny picture to make your friends laugh.

Extension: **them/him/her**

little

spider mouse bird dog rabbit ant

★ There was a **little** mouse in the story.

★

★

★

★

★

Draw a picture of your favourite book character.

Extension: **small/tiny**

Prim-Ed Publishing   www.prim-ed.com

Key Word Sentences 22

live

church   farm   garage   school   shop   hospital

★ I **live** next door to a school.

★

★

★

★

★

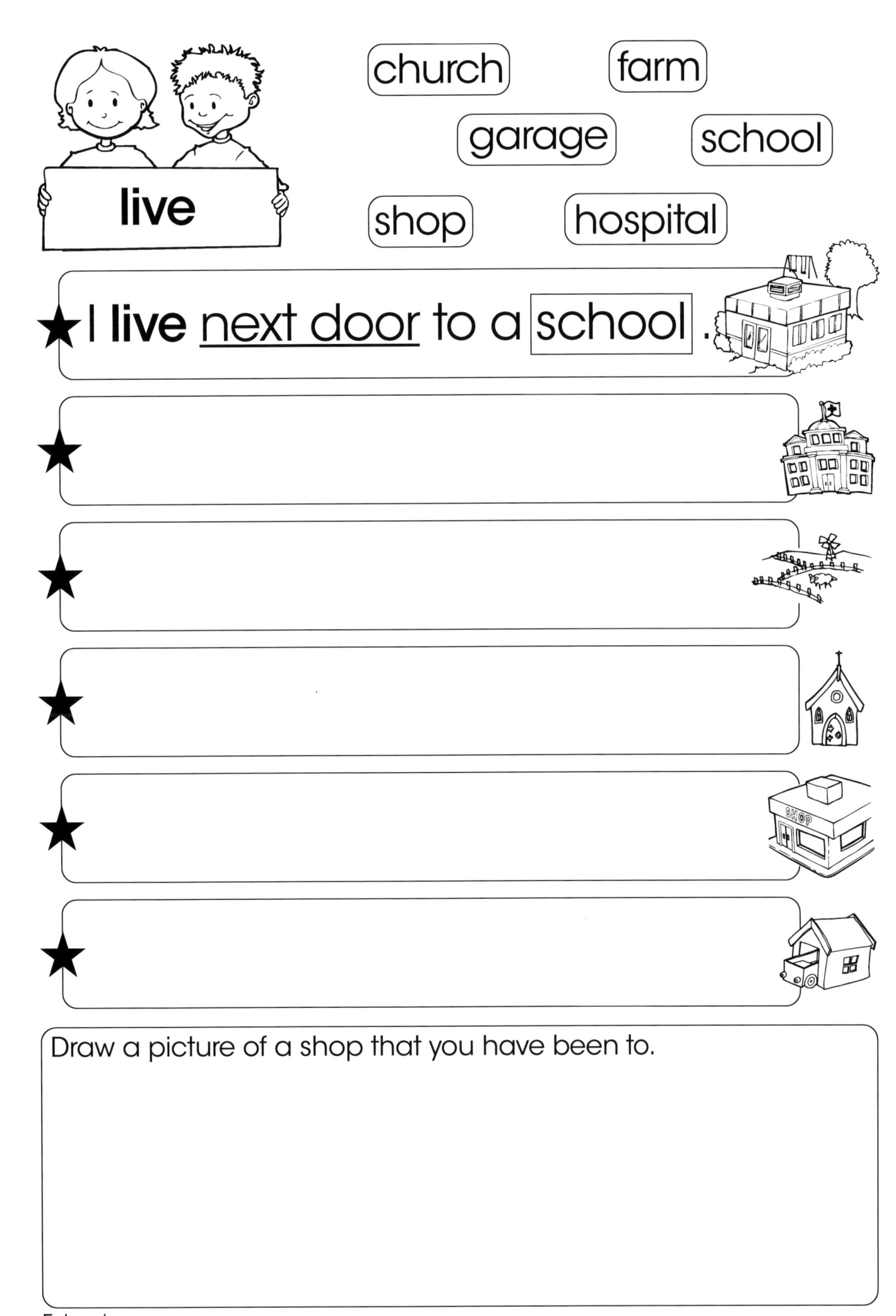

Draw a picture of a shop that you have been to.

Extension: **near**

lived

My best friend		in a flat.
Your mum		near the beach.
The dog	lived	in the town.
His grandma		next to the old woman.
We have		in a big house.
The family		next door.

★

★

★

★

★

★

Key Word Sentences 24

many

goats pigs sheep horses cows chickens

★ There are **many** cows on that farm.

★

★

★

★

★

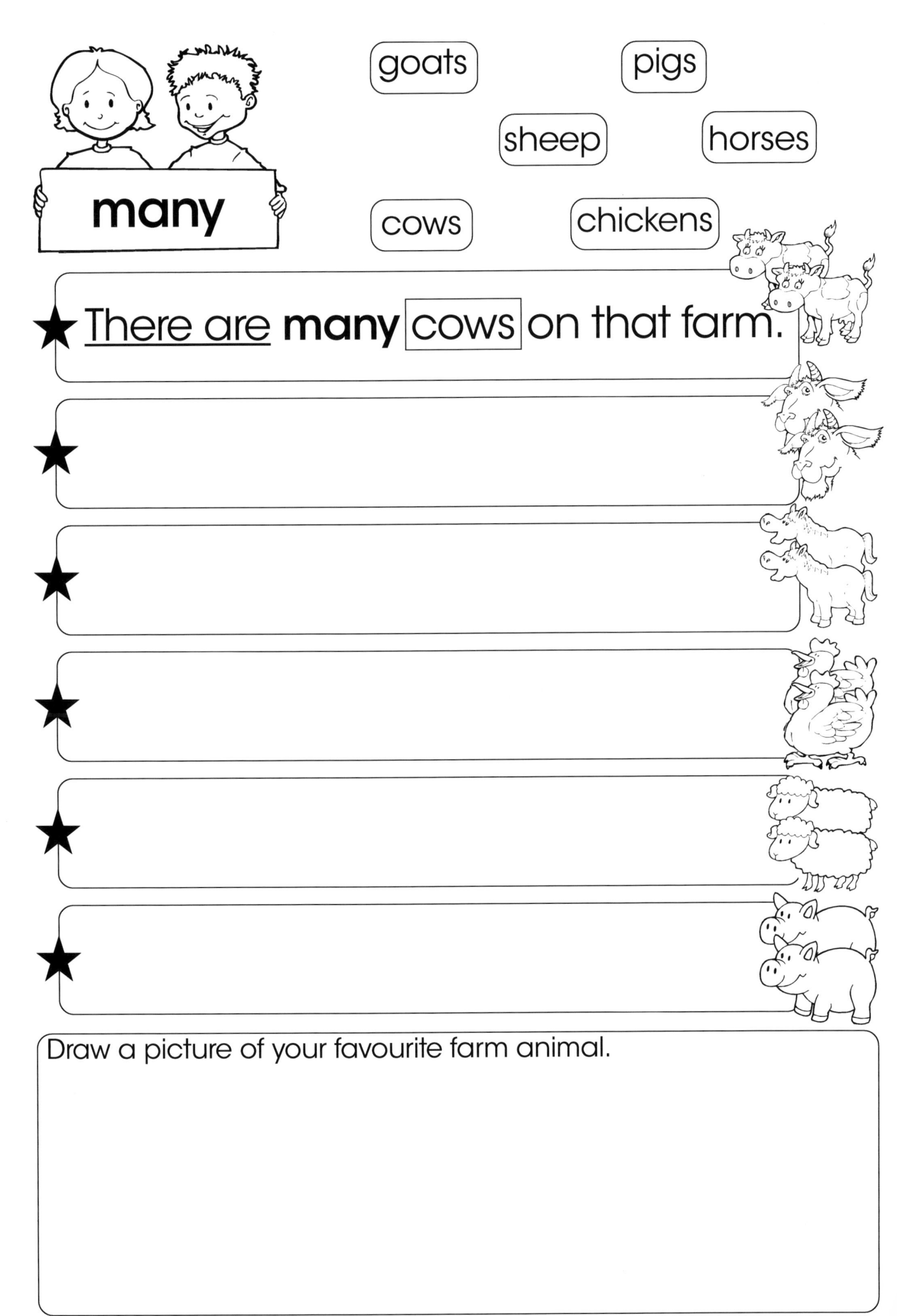

Draw a picture of your favourite farm animal.

Extension: **Are there …?/Will there be …?**

Prim-Ed Publishing www.prim-ed.com

Key Word Sentences 25

may

perfume purse gloves book brush hat

★ You **may** have her brush in your bag.

★

★

★

★

★

Design a bag.

Extension: **that/this**

Key Word Sentences 26

more

cherries   peas   chips   grapes   carrots   biscuits

★ I had **more** biscuits than my friend.

★

★

★

★

★

Draw your friend sharing your biscuits.

Extension: **have/want/bought**

birthday card letter
parcel postcard
Christmas card invitation

★ The **name** was on the invitation.

★

★

★

★

★

Draw a picture for a Christmas card.

Extension: **address/stamp**

new

teddy   dress
coat   ball
car   bike

★ I had a new bike last week.

★

★

★

★

★

Draw a picture of a bicycle.

Extension: **got/saw/bought**

Key Word Sentences 29

next

riding   shopping   swimming   skating   dancing   on holiday

★ I am going on holiday next week.

★

★

★

★

★

Draw yourself going shopping.

Extension: **might go/will go/can go**

night

At night	I can see the stars.
Every night	I go to bed.
	I go to sleep.
	I read a book.
	I brush my teeth.
	I have a bedtime story.

★
★
★
★
★
★

Key Word Sentences 31

old

woman   house
coin   chair
man   car

★ The man is very old.

★

★

★

★

★

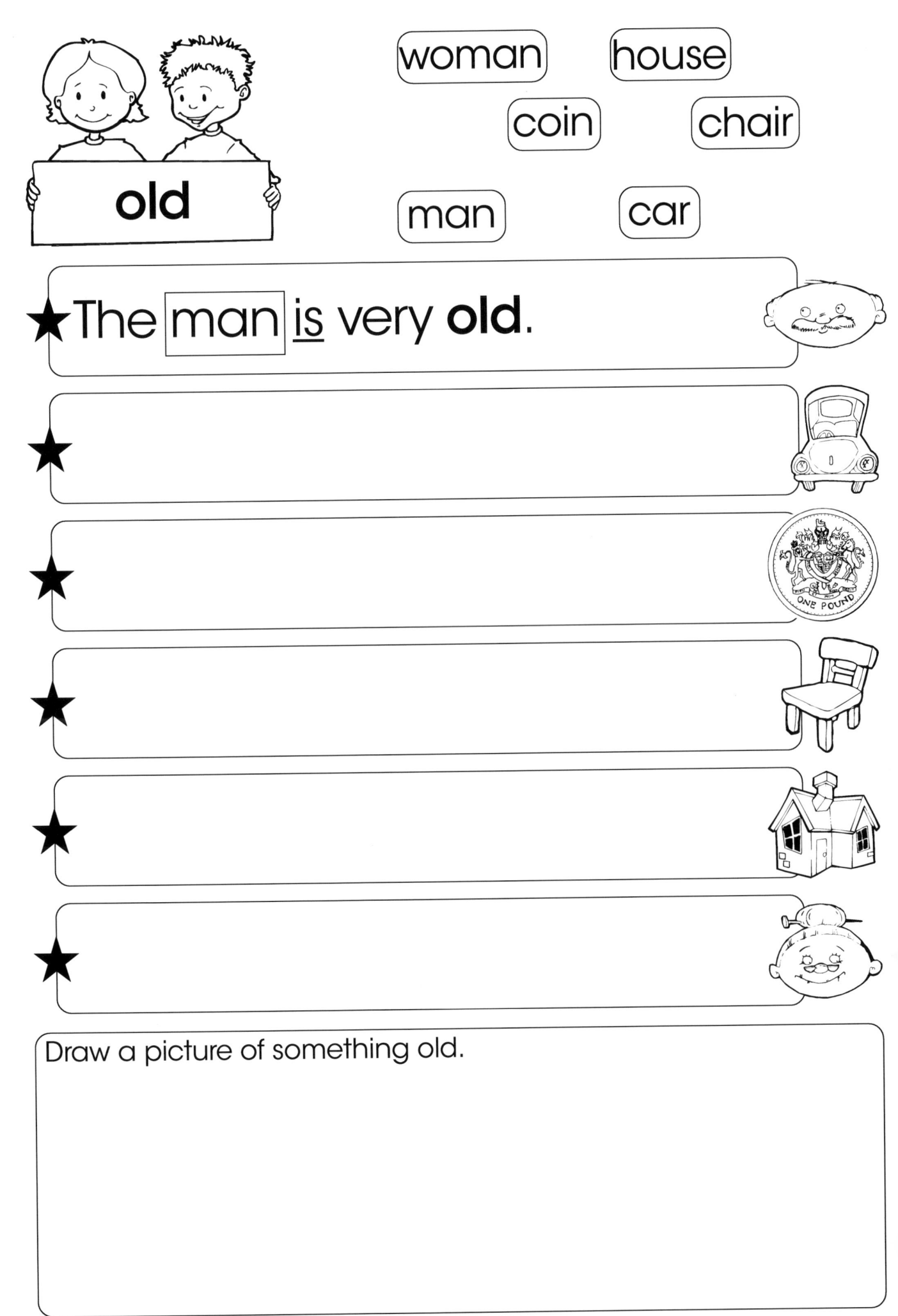

Draw a picture of something old.

Extension: **was / could be / might be**

Key Word Sentences 32

once

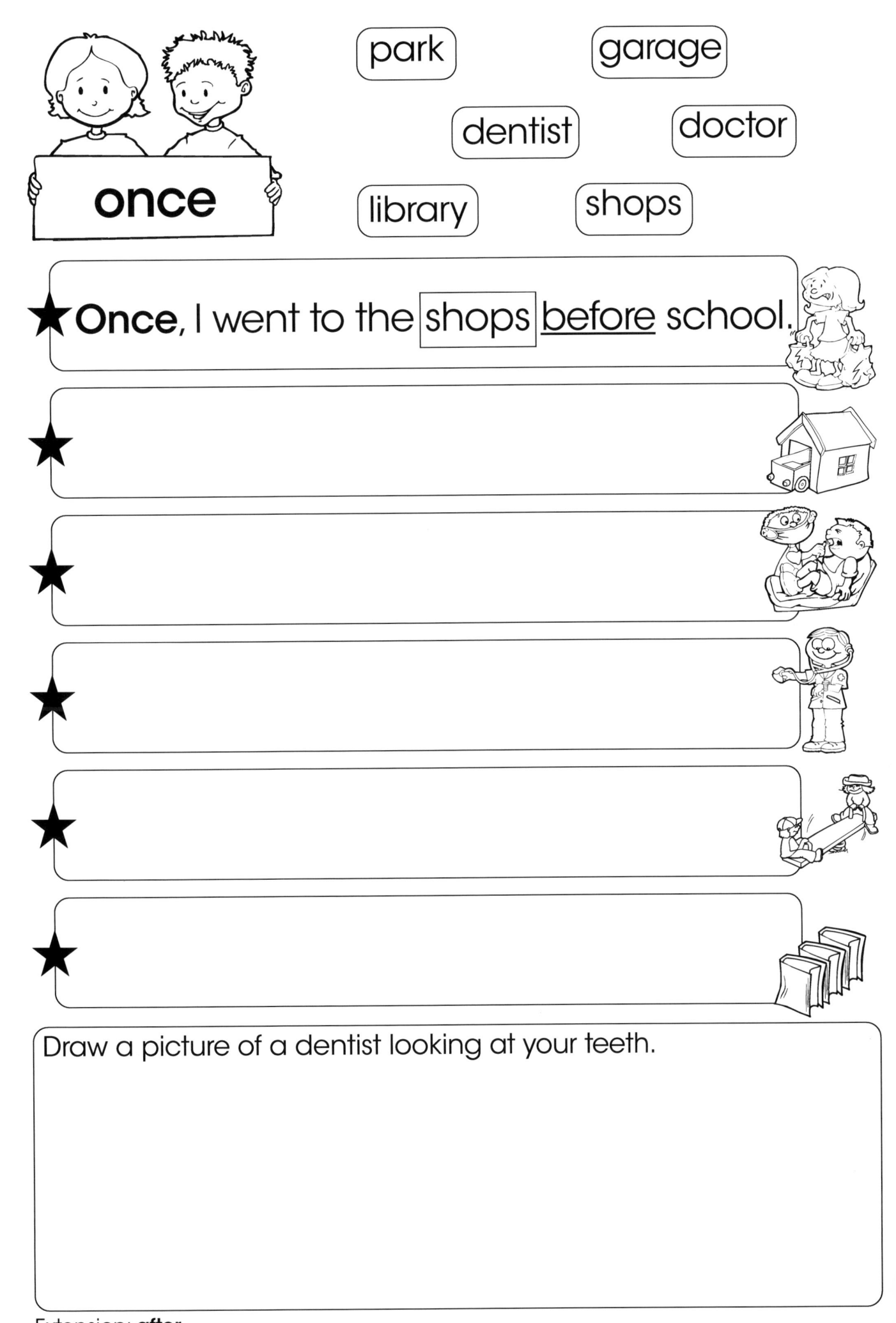

park garage dentist doctor library shops

★ **Once**, I went to the shops before school.

★

★

★

★

★

Draw a picture of a dentist looking at your teeth.

Extension: **after**

Key Word Sentences 33

our

sausages ice-cream fish spaghetti toast strawberries

★ My mum gives us strawberries for **our** tea.

★

★

★

★

★

Draw a big bowl of ice-cream.

Extension: **Your / His / Her / Their / Our**

Key Word Sentences 34

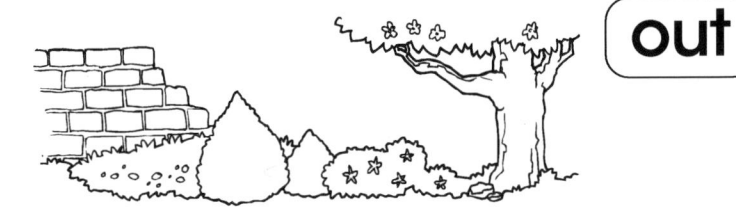

out

The man went	in the car.
My dad went	into the garden.
My friend went	after tea.
My mum went	with the dog.
Your sister went	to the shops.
Your brother went	for a walk.

★

★

★

★

★

★

over

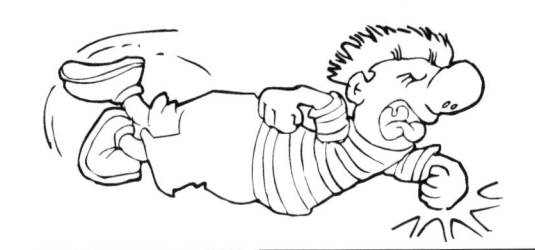

I fell over	my shoelace	and hurt my finger.
	the step	and hurt my knee.
	the ball	and hurt my foot.
	in the garden	and hurt my head.
	by the house	and hurt my back.
	when I was running	and hurt my elbow.

★

★

★

★

★

★

Key Word Sentences 36

people

coach   train
boat   plane
bus   bed

★ All the **people** got <u>on</u> the bus.

★

★

★

★

★

Draw a picture of lots of people on a train.

Extension: **off/onto**

pull

drawer window lid curtain cracker door

★ If I **pull** the door it will open.

★

★

★

★

★

Design some curtains.

Extension: **you/we/they**

push

My mum will push the wheelbarrow in the garden.

My mum can	our trolley in the supermarket.
My brother wanted to	my bike up the hill.
I helped my dad to	her on the swing.
I will try to	the pram.
My sister came to	me into a puddle.

★

★

★

★

★

★

Prim-Ed Publishing www.prim-ed.com

Key Word Sentences 39

saw

boy swing slide pond ball dog

★ At the park I **saw** a dog.

★

★

★

★

★

Draw a picture of children playing in the park.

Extension: will see / have seen / might see

Key Word Sentences 40

Prim-Ed Publishing www.prim-ed.com

school

draw write play read sing paint

★ At **school**, I like to [paint].

★

★

★

★

★

Draw yourself playing with your friends.

Extension: **home / my friend's house**

should

tomato banana orange pear carrot apple

★ You **should** eat <u>all</u> of your apple .

★

★

★

★

★

Draw a picture of the fruit you like to eat.

Extension: **some/most**

Key Word Sentences 42

sister

presents sandwich bag ring dress necklace

★ Your **sister** might <u>like</u> the necklace.

★

★

★

★

★

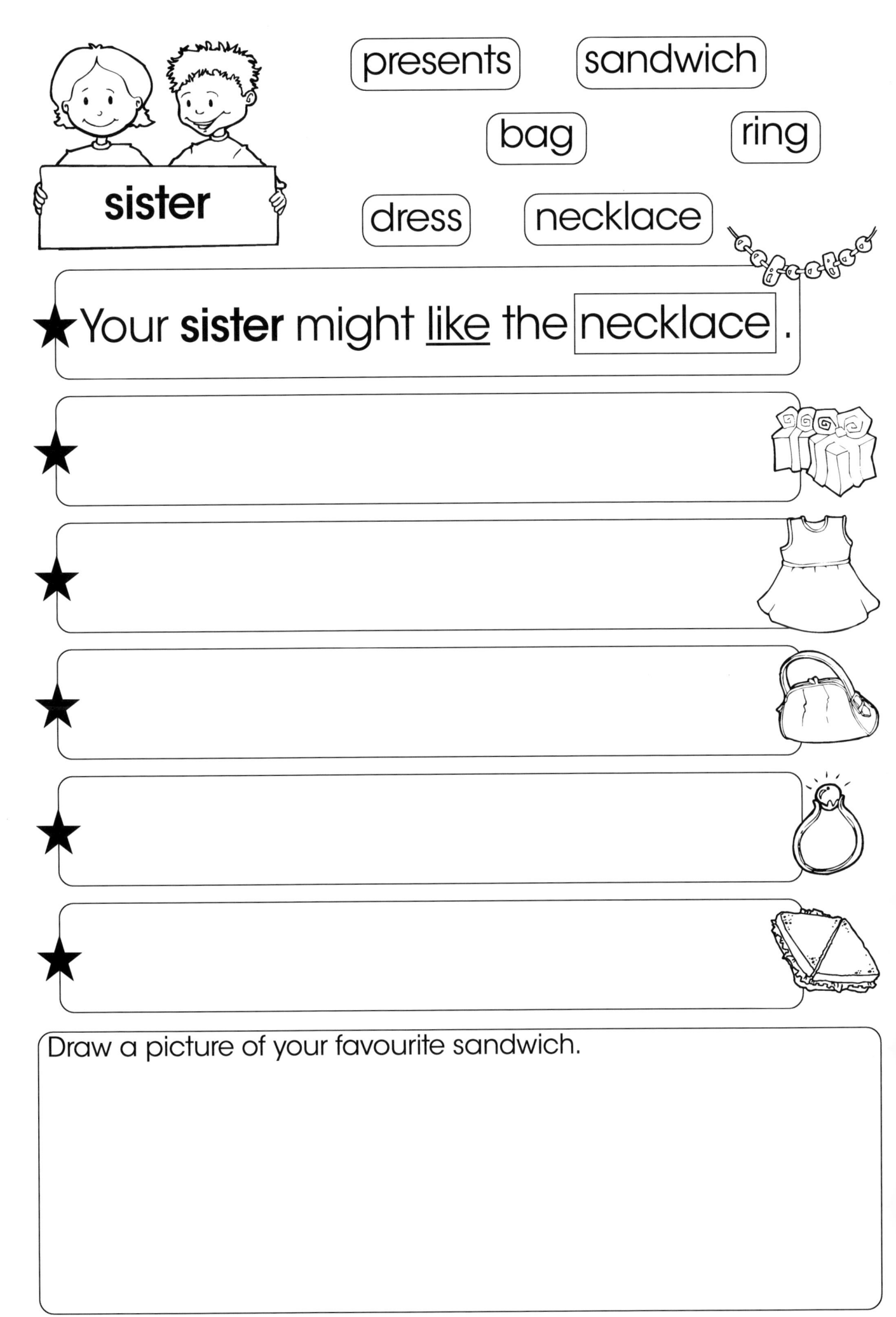

Draw a picture of your favourite sandwich.

Extension: **take / want / buy / find**

Key Word Sentences 43

some

fish   sausages   eggs   cheese   chips   beans

★ You can have **some** cheese.

★

★

★

★

★

Draw your favourite food.

Extension: **my / his / her / our / their**

take

flowers   newspaper   picture   sweets   bag   book

★ I <u>will</u> **take** the [book] home.

★

★

★

★

★

Draw a picture of flowers in a garden.

Extension: **can/might/would/could/should/may**

Key Word Sentences 45

than

books   crayons   toys   pencils   pets   chips

★ I have more chips than you.

★

★

★

★

★

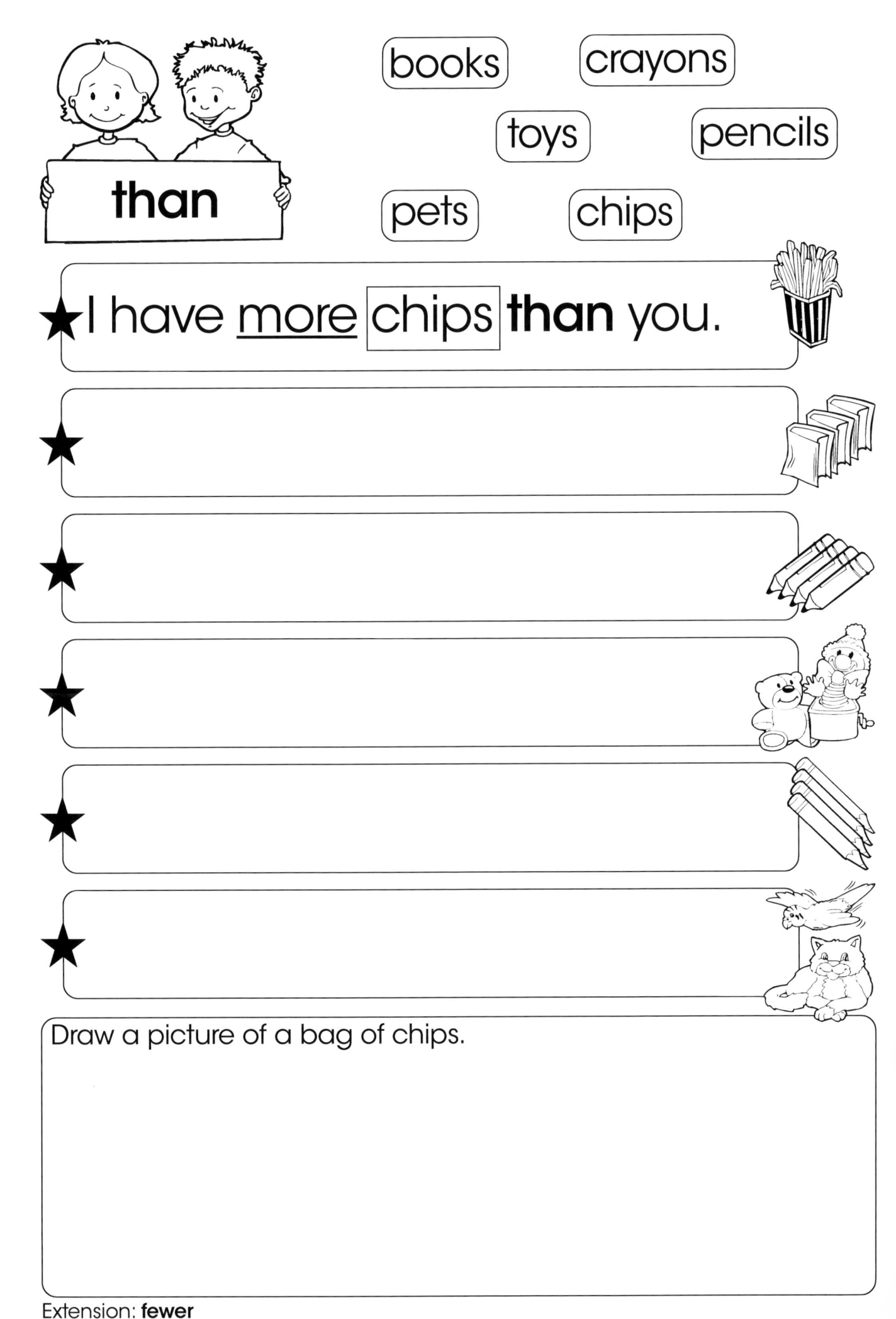

Draw a picture of a bag of chips.

Extension: **fewer**

Key Word Sentences 46

their

money   toothbrushes   glasses   shoes   rings   boots

★ They put **their** boots in the kitchen.

★

★

★

★

★

Draw a picture of your shoes.

Extension: **dropped/lost/found**

these

socks   scissors   gloves   apples   sausages   shoes

★ May I have **these** shoes ?

★

★

★

★

★

Draw a picture of your shoes.

Extension: **those**

three

benches   children   kites   ducks   dogs   balloons

★ I saw **three** dogs in the park.

★

★

★

★

★

Draw a picture of yourself playing in the park.

Extension: **four / five / six / seven / eight / nine / ten**

time

bed   breakfast   lunch   tea   school   swimmimg

★ It's **time** for tea.

★

★

★

★

★

Draw a picture of your school.

Extension: **Is it time for …?**

Key Word Sentences 50

too

coat   skirt
scarf   apron
bed   jumper

★ My jumper was **too** big for me.

★

★

★

★

★

Draw a picture of yourself wearing a very long scarf.

Extension: **small/long/short**

took

station post office pool house shops party

★ Anna **took** her friend to the party.

★

★

★

★

★

Draw a picture of your house.

Extension: **walked/drove**

Key Word Sentences 52

kite   ball
boy   girl
tree
balloon   cat

★ The cat got stuck in <u>the</u> **tree**.

★

★

★

★

★

Design a kite.

Extension: **my / our / your / his / her / their**

water

tap kettle vase bath jug cup

★ There is **water** in <u>the</u> cup .

★

★

★

★

★

Draw a picture with water in it.

Extension: your / my / his / her / that / this

Key Word Sentences 54

way

car   bus   bicycle   house   train   dog

★ On the **way** to school I saw a dog.

★

★

★

★

★

Draw something you have seen on the way to school.

Extension: **home/to the shops**

Key Word Sentences 55

Who

shed   street   kitchen   garage   garden   shop

★ **Who** was <u>in the</u> shop ?

★

★

★

★

★

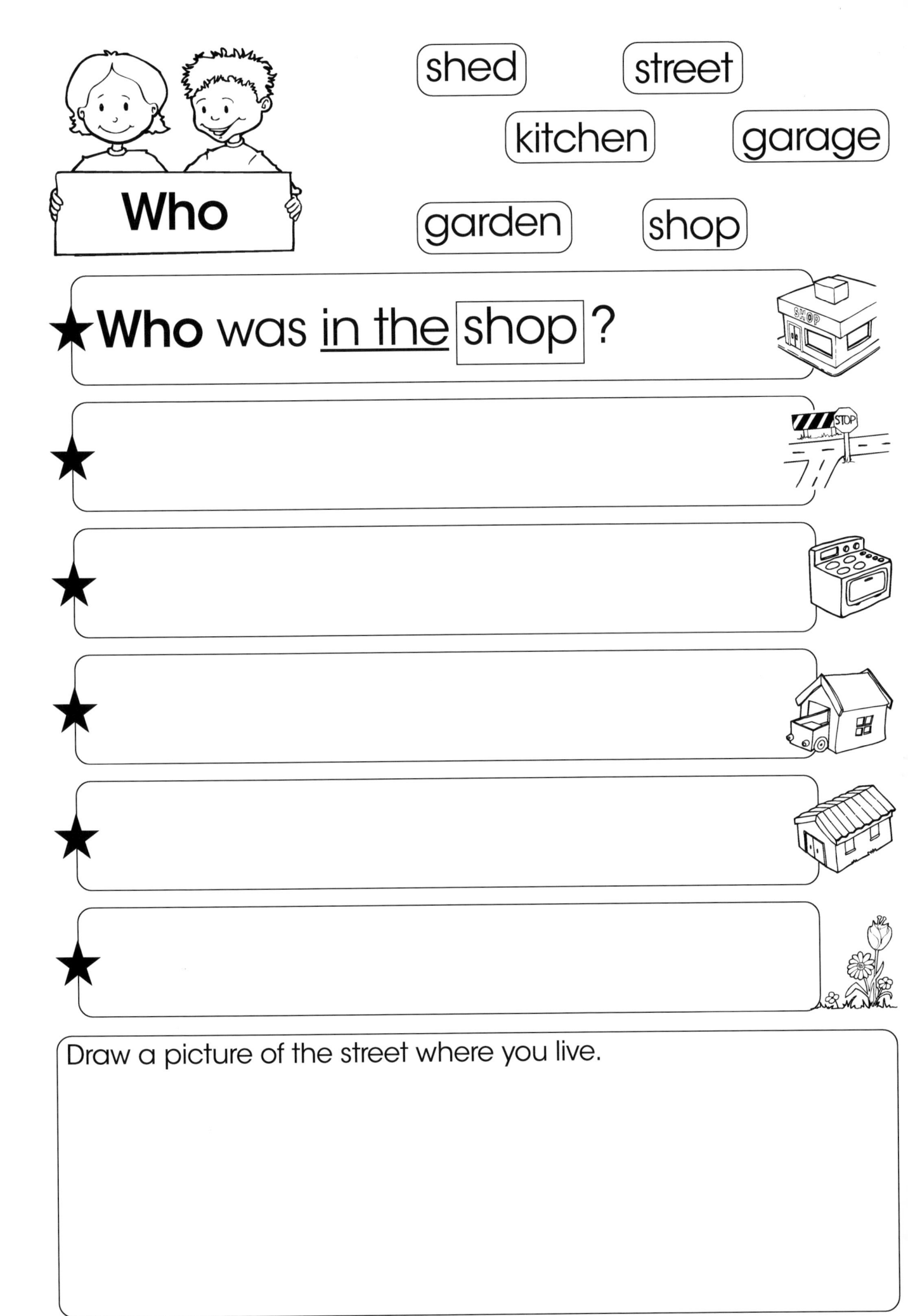

Draw a picture of the street where you live.

Extension: **at the ...park/party/fair/circus**

Prim-Ed Publishing www.prim-ed.com

Key Word Sentences 56

would

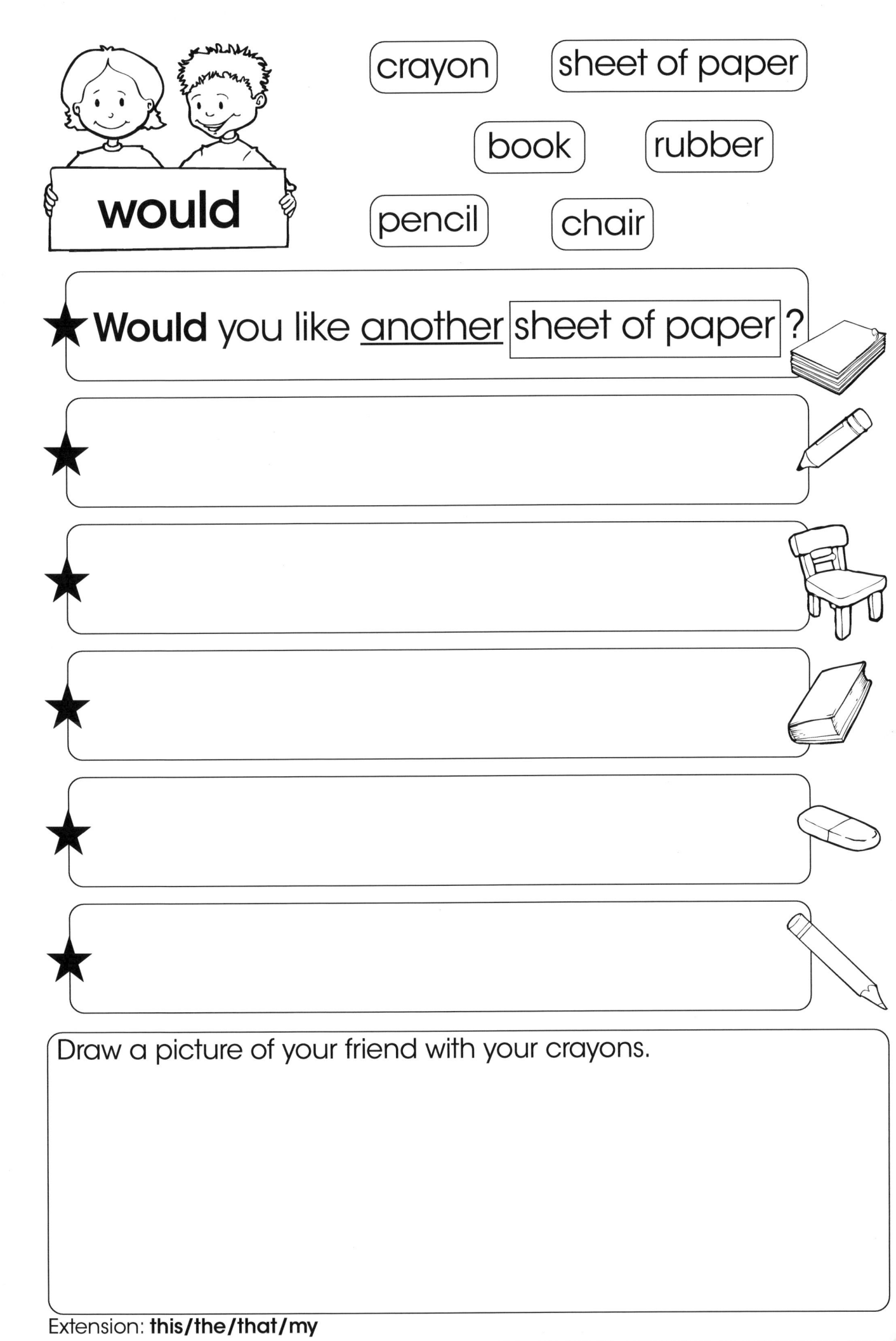

crayon   sheet of paper

book   rubber

pencil   chair

★ **Would** you like <u>another</u> sheet of paper ?

★

★

★

★

★

Draw a picture of your friend with your crayons.

Extension: **this / the / that / my**